WILD OPPOSITION

THE BEATITUDES OF JESUS *AND* THE TRANSFORMED LIFE

TIM FEARER

2022

ISBN: 9798747315082

Photos:
Open Book by Unknown
Double Take by Pouria Teymouri
Jesus Saves by Patricia McCarty
Poor in Spirit (wrecked church) by Unknown
Mourn by Brian James
Meek by Suzy Hazelwood
Filled by Maria Orlova
Interlude by Amine M'Siouri
Merciful by Madeline Bassinder
Pure in Heart by Deepan Karthick
Peacemakers by Tima Miroshnichenko
Persecuted by Swapnil Sharm

Cover photo by Amine M'Siouri

Back cover photo by Pouria Teymouri

for my nephews – Sam, Nate and Gabe,
this book is for them and their generation

You Christians have in your hands a book containing enough dynamite to shatter civilization.

Mahatma Gandhi

The adult members of society adverted to the Bible unreasonably often . . . If they had read it, I thought, they would have hid it. They didn't recognize the vivid danger that we would, through repeated exposure, catch a case of its wild opposition to their world.

Annie Dillard
An American Childhood

The Beatitudes are better heard as Jesus' pronouncements of radical grace, not a list of virtues. It is a Kingdom in which the most unlikely may be blessed and become the "light of the world."

N.T. Wright

TABLE OF CONTENTS

PART I

PREPARING FOR THE WORDS

THE PROBLEM

Jesus' Beatitudes . . . they must be important. In his most famous speech this is where he starts. These are the first words out his mouth. And somebody bothered to write them down.

The words, phrases and images pulse with life and hope. They're quotable, memorable, suitable for framing. But what do they mean?

And how do we take them as a whole? Their connection with each other appears like beads gathered off the floor and strung together without a thought. They're a riddle, a puzzle.

This little book is my take on the riddle and the puzzle. Much of the content is not original to me. I rely on plenty of others.

What I'm offering is a way to read Jesus' words of blessing that makes the most sense, the best sense, given what precedes them, what follows them and how they progress.

They wind up being a story, of all things! The story of a transformed life. That life upends the world and then blesses it.

That life, that story can be yours.

Tim Fearer

Winter 2022 / Ventura, California

THE WORDS THEMSELVES

[3]*'Blessed are the poor in spirit, for theirs is the kingdom of heaven.*

[4]*'Blessed are those who mourn, for they will be comforted.*

[5]*'Blessed are the meek, for they will inherit the earth.*

[6]*'Blessed are those who hunger and thirst for righteousness, for they will be filled.*

[7]*'Blessed are the merciful, for they will receive mercy.*

[8]*'Blessed are the pure in heart, for they will see God.*

[9]*'Blessed are the peacemakers, for they will be called children of God.'*

[10]*'Blessed are those who are persecuted for righteousness' sake, for theirs is the kingdom of heaven.'*

[11] *'Blessed are you when people revile you and persecute you and utter all*
kinds of evil against you falsely on my account. [12]*Rejoice and be glad, for*
your reward is great in heaven, for in the same way they persecuted the
prophets who were before you.'

Matthew 5:3-12 *(New Revised Standard Version)*

DOING A DOUBLE TAKE

WHAT ARE THEY?

Beatitudes. When you first hear them, you don't know what to make of them.

We sat semi-attentive in Sunday school. They were stated, then repeated, almost in an off-handed way. Declared to us against a backdrop of unapologetic, worldly success. No one seemed aware of, let alone admitted the irony, the juxtaposed rivalry. Annie Dillard put it this way – "staggering texts" read to us "sweet mouthed and earnest."

Beatitudes. We were inoculated against them with controlled doses. We recognized no dissonance, as if nothing was supposed to happen in response. No questions, no challenge, no decision on our part. No unavoidable step out of the world we both inhabited and loved, and then into another.

Others of us heard them like a foreign language. They came as snippets out of context. We had no church or cultural background to locate them. They infiltrated where they didn't belong. They showed up in a sitcom, in a love song, in a violent movie. They spoke, like some party crasher breaking up the chit chat with a proverb.

We let them pass by. We didn't run after them, as if they weren't really addressing us. As if they were not looking us square in the eye. As if they were not a call.

Even in the midst of a disruptive, God-saturated social movement that was sweeping a younger version of me and my generation into the arms of Jesus, we still didn't quite hear them. They made no coherent sense. They made no difference. Nobody opened them up.

But then they continue speaking. Something clicks. This time they call you by name. They require that you stop, look and listen. Really listen. And you don't know what to do with them. You don't know how to respond to them. But for the first time, you hear them.

You hear when you're ready to hear.

NOT WHAT WE THOUGHT

Beatitudes. Jesus is not sitting us down and giving us a lecture on morals. Jesus is not boiling down Christianity into something all religions share. And Jesus is not doing his best to make good people better.

Jesus' Beatitude words are not random opinions offered scatter-shot for special case people. They are not a thoughtful nod to the down and out, as opposed to the rest of us. And they are not a domesticated, declawed, housebroken Jesus getting harmlessly philosophical.

Jesus' words are not a self-help, self-improvement, empowerment manual. They are not eight ways toward greater satisfaction. Jesus is not baptizing your pre-set obligations and commitments, and then supplementing them with sanctimonious advice for you in your off-hours.

This is not getting in touch with the god within. This is not an appeal nor an ode to human potential. It is not a celebration of our "better angels."

And this is not at all what the self-serving voices are saying in a steady drumbeat through every activated device you own.

This is not what you were taught, not what you have believed, not what you have based your life upon and benefited from.

No. Instead, this is a radical questioning of all of that. This is a direct assault on all of that.

Beatitudes. Jesus is sending a shot over the bow. He is shelling the beach and then landing on it. This is an attack upon the best defenses of the world system outside of you and within you.

It knocks you off your feet like an explosion. It makes collateral damage out of all who cling to "their way" of looking at things. It devastates the invincible and the proud.

At first blush it seems innocent enough. It sounds like a sympathetic "there, there" for a life that has taken a bad turn. It looks like a condescending "try to be good" to those with nothing better to do. But then it turns out to be shock therapy, repeated jolts to the brain reaching down and into the heart.

Jesus' Beatitude words are nothing less than a shakedown, turning the "System" upside down and watching it come apart. It reveals what really is there and what is not.

Jesus' Beatitude words are a complete unmasking of a pretend and brittle world arrayed against God.

NOT SO FAST

Are the people here "blessed"? Yes, they are. Again, and again, blessed. "Blessed" is the repeated, unquestioned, common thread that holds these lines together. That's good news, but not so fast. No good news without bad news.

Oh, this is all about the greatest and deepest and most enduring blessedness one could ever hope for and then possess. But it doesn't always come with a gentle knock on the door.

When you hear it, it may rap and bang. And when you open up, even just a crack, it can rush in and start breaking things. The teardown, the remodel, the new furniture are better than you would ever have imagined. But the process can be convulsive.

These are some of the words better associated with what Jesus' Beatitudes are doing to our cherished order – bulldoze, flatten, dismantle, devastate, annihilate, obliterate, crush, raze, wreck, ruin, trash, pulverize, broadside, blast, blitz, barrage, bombardment, cannonade, fusillade, demolish, torpedo, sink.

Is this too much? Too negative? I don't think so, not until you get the message. This is a dead reckoning, after all. This is an overthrow – a final and subversive undermining of all that currently claims absolute and ultimate sway.

This is not a momentary breath of fresh air, a welcomed afternoon breeze clearing the haze on an otherwise sunny day. No, this is a hurricane leveling all that cannot stand, all that is built on sand rather than rock:

- entire civilizations founded on a false premise;

- cardboard movie sets blown down and revealed to be flimsy, two-dimensional fakes;
- you and me.

This is a prairie fire. This is scorched earth.

But look what grows out of the ashes! Blessing.

Beatitude – from the Latin *beatus* meaning blessed, happy, fortunate, prosperous. "Supreme blessedness."

FIRST THINGS FIRST

There is no blessing without prior demolition. Jesus has to clear the way, clear the ground of all that would get in the way, all that would keep you from life as God intended it.

This is a vision of life. This is life in the Kingdom of Heaven, embodied in the one who himself promises and delivers it.

But in the midst of that and all along the way it is a wrecking ball. A blessed, heavenly wrecking ball.

First it knocks down what is left of feeble, hollow, defiant you. Then it builds you back up with blessing after blessing into someone solid and enduring and full of life.

And then as you begin living that life two things happen. First, you spread that life around. Second, as you do, you have that same blessed wrecking ball effect on all that is false around you.

I didn't know Jesus' "blessed" words would make you a subversive, an insurgent, a blessed leveler of entire neighborhoods. I didn't know you would become an infectious spreader of life, unmasking the culture of death in your vicinity, getting you harassed, beat up, jailed, even killed.

I didn't know, let alone believe, any of that.

Now I do.

SETTING IT ALL UP

THE BACKDROP

Jesus of Nazareth has died to himself in baptism. He has surrendered to his "Father." And with that, because of that, he is simultaneously empowered and authorized.

Immediately he is led into the wilderness, tempted by the devil, stress-tested by God. He passes.

Now he's ready.

He emerges from the wilderness and sets up a base of operations. Settles in a fishing village called Capernaum (ke-PUR-nay-em) on the north shore of the Sea of Galilee (GA-le-lee). He begins preaching his heart out and collecting disciples. (See Matthew 3:13—4:22.)

Then we get this:

[23]Jesus went throughout Galilee, teaching in their synagogues and proclaiming the good news of the kingdom and curing every disease and every sickness among the people.

[24]So his fame spread throughout all Syria, and they brought to him all the sick, those who were afflicted with various diseases and pains, demoniacs, epileptics, and paralytics, and he cured them. [25]And great crowds followed him from Galilee, the Decapolis, Jerusalem, Judea, and from beyond the Jordan.

Matthew 4:23-25

The whole thing catches fire.

Jesus of Nazareth – coming out of Nazareth, coming out of nowhere – commands immediate attention, shakes it all up, and draws people like a magnet.

Initially he wanders around a backwater region, surprising everyone with what he says and what he can do. Now "great crowds" from every corner of the map are searching for him, converging and pressing in upon him.

Jesus is going viral.

Jesus is like a wandering bonfire igniting every tinder-dry thing around him in a non-stop blaze of preaching, teaching, healings and exorcisms!

What is this?

This is nothing less than the Kingdom of Heaven. The Kingdom has arrived, and this is what it looks like.

THE EFFECT

I don't know about you, but that kind of action interests me. If that's "church," I want to be a part of it. I want to sign up for something like that.

As a matter of fact, I did sign up for something like that when I said "Yes" to Jesus Christ in my youth. I and many in my generation were swept up by this Jesus. We were gathered up by the God he spoke of. We were lifted up by an uncompromising message of love, mercy and forgiveness poured out upon our lives.

It was and is a message breaking the strangle hold of sin and death. It was and is a message of God's justice making things right. It was and is a message of power.

That power would take my life and turn it into something beautiful for him. That power would change me – an insecure and troubled middle school student at the time – into someone God wanted to use for his beyond-my-imagination purposes.

As best as I understood it at the time, I said Yes to all that. I wrapped my arms around that. I wrapped my life around a day-by-day journey with him – a moment by moment Yes, Yes, and forever-after Yes to him.

THE CRISIS

A funny thing happens in the story at this point. With the fires of this awakening burning in Galilee, Jesus pushes the pause button. Jesus calls a time out and walks off the field. He walks away, temporarily, but he does walk away.

Why does Jesus walk away?

Let's keep reading and see what we find.

[1]When he saw the crowds, he went up the mountain; and after he sat down, his disciples came to him. [2]Then he began to speak, and taught them, saying: [3]'Blessed are the poor in spirit, for theirs is the kingdom of heaven.'
Matthew 5:1-3

Why would Jesus walk away when everything is going right, with his popularity cresting, with the crowds ready to follow him anywhere?

What would make Jesus stop this thing dead in its tracks and wander off?

THE TURN

I believe the answer to the previous question is found in the first five words of verse 1:

> *When he saw the crowds . . .*

We typically breeze by and ignore this, but it's not there by accident. What do these five words have to do with Jesus' on-fire ministry we just read about (4:23-25) and the Sermon on the Mount (chs. 5—7) which follows?

This was not the first time Jesus has seen the crowds. He's been seeing them all along in recent days and weeks. This is nothing new. So why the five words?

Here's my expanded paraphrase of 5:1-2 with my understanding of the first five words and their significance:

> *When he saw the crowds **again**... when he saw the masses of people and their relentless and pressing need, when he considered the sheer numbers and that there was only one of him, he stopped. He stopped, withdrew with those who were close to him, and headed up the side of the adjacent highlands.*
>
> *When they got far enough away from the crowds he sat down. Then his core people gathered around him, **and he started giving his ministry away to them.***

After all, he had said to Peter and Andrew earlier as they left their nets, "Follow me, and I will make you fish for people" (Matthew 4:19). Now it begins.

And as Jesus speaks, he is saying to them in so many words something like this:

> *"Before this thing goes any further, let's understand each other. If you want to be with me, if you want a share in what I'm doing, if you want to do the things I'm doing, you've got to get this down. You've got to take the things I am about to say to you, wrap your arms around them, accept them, believe and begin living into them."*
>
> *"You've got to get these words inside of you, so they become a part of you, become second nature to you and begin to change you. You've got to let God change the way you think so God can change the way you are! Otherwise, you can forget about being with me and having a share in what I am doing."*

The crowds are overwhelming – too many people, too many demands. The ministry will collapse under its own weight and crush him. Time to develop the people around him and begin placing the ministry into their hands. This was his plan all along. This is that story.

And this story is our story, as well.

FROM THE MOUNTAIN

Matthew writes with a Jewish audience in mind. Lots of references to the Hebrew Scriptures. None of it needs translation for the hearers. (Compare the *Gospel of Mark* on both counts, written for Gentiles.)

Is Matthew casting Jesus as the new Moses?

- This is the only gospel with Jesus as a threatened but divinely protected infant with a season in Egypt (Exodus 2; Matthew 2).

- Five sections of teaching are found in Matthew. The first five books of the Old Testament are traditionally referred to as the "Books of Moses."

- Both Moses' and Jesus' give definitive teachings delivered from mountains. Jesus' new "law" comments on, deepens and, at times, creatively adjusts the law of Moses.

The new Moses? Why not? Then again, he's more than Moses.

TAKING A SEAT

Before Jesus speaks, he sits down. This is the position of teaching authority. Like in the synagogue – you stand up to read the scripture, then sit down to teach. It's like in the boat just off the beach in Mark 4 and Luke 5. There he sits, the rabbi teaching the crowds.

And in the Greek text of Matthew 5:2 there is trigger language associated with one who has authority to teach. It literally says, "opening his mouth" (a traditional, technical phrase signaling that teaching is about to come) "he began to teach them, saying . . .."

WHEN WE HEAR "BLESSED"

"Blessed." "I'm blessed." "I'm so blessed." What does that mean?

In current culture it's usually a "how I'm doing" summarizer.

It can also be a wrap up, once evidence has been offered, proving one's blessed status in the universe. For example, showing pictures of the grandkids with the conclusion "I'm so blessed."

Or "I'm blessed" can be a teaser inviting inquiry. "Really? Tell me more."

Or "I'm blessed" can be a conversation stopper, shorthand for "Life is good. I have family and friends around me, material comforts, money in the bank, a healthy body, promising outlook, etc., but I don't want to get into those details right now."

By the way, God is not necessarily included in any of these equations.

As far as all that goes, "I'm blessed" resembles some of what we pick up when the word "bless" or "blessed" is used in the Hebrew Scriptures (Old Testament).

"BLESSED" IN THE HEBREW SCRIPTURES

In the Hebrew Scriptures "bless," "blessing," "blessed" are tied to earthly existence and one's condition in it with material and relational realities well ordered.

At their core "bless," "blessing," "blessed" are all about being fully alive and in abundance. When God blesses a person in the Hebrew Scriptures it is an impartation of life. It is an infusion of vital power and its benefits upon a person now and in all dimensions of one's existence. It even reaches into future generations as one's life is extended in the form of descendants. (See Genesis 12:1-3.)

On the occasions when one human being blesses another, it is a transfer of life and its power from the blesser to the blessed, for example, from father to son. (See Genesis 27-1-29.)*

WHEN JESUS SAYS "BLESSED"

Jesus uses the word "blessed" nine times In Matthew 5 and it's all right up front in the first ten verses.

As he says "blessed," he is not just making some wishful pronouncement. No, as he does, Jesus is calling down the life-giving power of God in all of its benefits and dimensions upon those to whom it applies.

Jesus is saying, "How blessed," that is," how favored, how divinely advantaged are you!"

And this state of blessedness is given a scope beyond what it possessed previously in the Old Testament.

---

*Outside of typical usage is the phrase "bless the LORD." Here blessing the LORD is paralleled with "praising" the LORD. It is to verbally make much of, "magnify," and ascribe appropriate laud and honor to God for all of his works in all of his glory. (See Psalm 34:1-3; see also Psalm 103.)

Further, this blessedness descends upon those who would never have been previously thought to be recipients. In fact, it is just the opposite!

But now we're getting ahead of ourselves. Let's get into the first word of blessing!

JESUS
SAVES

PART II

JESUS' BEATITUDE WORDS

ONCE AGAIN

Remember, Jesus sits everybody down for a heart-to-heart talk, a defining conversation, a literal "come to Jesus" moment. He is redrawing the map, re-defining reality, sketching out God's view of a blessed person and a blessed life.

This is a vision of a person and what life can be. It is a vision of what it must be, "If you want to be with me," he says.

It is disruptive and healing all at once.

It begins with a death.

I

BLESSED: ALL-POSSESSING EMPTY ONES

3 'Blessed are the poor in spirit,
for theirs is the kingdom of heaven.'

Matthew 5:3

POOR IN SPIRIT

You've got to be kidding. "The spiritually poor"? Those whose lives are in shambles, who have come to the end of themselves with nothing to show but reversal and failure?

This had traditionally been a sign of being abandoned by God, unconfessed and chronic selfishness, moral failure, unfit, unclean, something the matter.

Now this is presented as something positive, an advantage . . . something even to strive for?

Not something to strive for, but rather something to admit. Time to face the music about yourself. Time to strip off the make-up. Time to remove the mask.

Not everyone can hear that. Not everyone wants to do that. Not everyone can bear that.

We are in such a state of denial.

THE SPIN

Reality – life is not found where you think it is. The world does not work the way you think it does. It doesn't run according to the way you were taught and have believed and based your life upon.

The world around us says:

- "Blessed are the beautiful."

- "Blessed are the gifted."
- "Blessed are the privileged, and the rich, and the affluent."
- "Blessed are the strong."
- "Blessed are those in power and in positions of power."

After all, it is "survival of the fittest," isn't it? It is "dog eat dog," "let the best man win," let "the cream rise to the top." And you'd better be the cream, or you're going to wind up with nothing, a loser on all counts.

Blessed are those who passed the test, who made the grade, who didn't blink, who did it themselves. Pull yourself together, for God's sake! Pull yourself up by your own bootstraps! God helps those who help themselves! Not the faltering, not the struggling, not the weak.

And blessed are those who even if they failed, got back up again, took what was theirs and seized the victory!

If there is a God, such are the marks of God's blessing and his blessed ones. It's winner take all.

And in some conservative corners, in some church circles we may hear this: "Blessed are those with a squeaky-clean track record, with no moral flaws, no besetting sins, no slip ups, no guilt and no regrets. Those are the winners. Those are the blessed ones."

All that, by and large, is what the world around us is saying on a non-stop audio loop.

And if we're honest, that is what the world within us, embedded in our own hearts is saying.

And we've bought it.

THE SHOCKING TRUTH

But now Jesus Christ sits down with his followers and tells them something completely different. Something strange. Something foreign. Something counter-intuitive that doesn't rely on us but finds itself completely in God.

Jesus says this, "The Kingdom of Heaven, that is, everything you see me doing and everything I am about, belongs to one group of people – the spiritually bankrupt. It belongs to them and to nobody else. Them and them alone, period."

He says, "What the world has been telling you is a lie. It is a manipulative, unforgiving lie."

Are you tired of being lied to?

Are you tired of people trying to sell you something?

Here is Jesus Christ with a shocking statement, with a stunning truth, with a lifegiving, refreshing, completely unexpected kind of reality.

He says,

- "Blessed are the ones who have *not* made it!"
- "Blessed are those who are broken and know it."
- "Blessed are the ones on the ground and face down."
- "Blessed are those whose plans and expectations have crumbled, whose hopes and dreams have come to nothing."
- "Blessed are the passed over, pushed aside and unfavored."

- "Blessed are those of no regard."
- "Blessed are those at the end of their rope."

He's not done.

- "Blessed are those who *have* 'made it,' but in their affluent emptiness see clearly now that the world has not, will not and cannot deliver on its promises."
- "Blessed are those who see they have been sold a bill of goods."
- "Blessed are those, rich or poor, who have come to terms with themselves, who know they are inadequate, who know they are full of sin and selfishness, who know that left to themselves there *is no hope.*"

HOW HAPPY!

Jesus again, "How happy are such people, God bless them! God bless you, because the Kingdom of Heaven is yours!"

"Everything that you see in me, everything you see me doing and giving to the crowds:

- full and abundant life,
- a healed life,
- a changed life,
- purpose in life in the here and the now and in the hereafter with all of its rights, its privileges, and its responsibilities . . .

. . . all this belongs to the ones who let go of all the lies and all the spin, who let go of the fantasy and open their hands and open their hearts and embrace this truth:

> *"Blessed are the poor in spirit."*

The Kingdom of Heaven belongs not to the proud, not to the self-sufficient, not to the self-secured, not to the defiantly self-righteous.

It belongs to the desperate and the discouraged and the broken-hearted.

THE BEGINNING POINT

"For those who want to be with me," Jesus says, "this is where you begin. There is no other place to start.

"The beginning point is not talent, it is not social advantage, nor merit, nor the luck of the draw, nor class, nor achievement.

"The beginning point with me is this – the mercy of God and the grace of God poured upon your broken life.

"And if you don't believe that, and I mean not just believe it up here [he points to his holy head], but actually gamble your life upon that . . . If you don't start with me in that place, if you don't wrap your arms around and embrace that truth, then you really have nothing to do with me.

"And in that case, you can't be *with* me, and you certainly can't do my ministry."

PERFECT SPECIMEN

I was talking with this young guy several years ago – an average, run of the mill person like you and me. I invited him to consider serving the church we were both in by becoming a teacher of the Bible.

He had real ability. He had desire. People responded to him every time he shared something from what he had been reading.

But when I ran the idea by him, he resisted the suggestion. He said to me, "You know, Tim, I'm a spiritually broken person."

I knew his story. I knew his struggles – past, present, ongoing. I responded and said, "Yeah, that's true. And that's why I am talking to you. You're just the kind of person Jesus Christ is looking for."

That's right.

Do you believe that?

THE LONELINESS OF MOST CHURCHES

Most churches are full of pretend, because they are full of people.

We pretend because we are afraid. We are afraid of being truly known, found out. And once we are known and found out, then we are going to be disqualified and rejected and excluded from the religious club. Cut from the herd.

That's how we think. And a lot of churches do work that way. We put on the mask and put on the show. We wear our achievements. We hide the other stuff.

We settle for the loneliness and the isolation of being unknown, because we think it is safe. This way we can be accepted and loved, if you want to call it that.

I want you to know my best side, my best efforts and accomplishments, the person I want you to think that I am. I can manage that program well, and I can manage you. Then I get from you that pseudo-love and acceptance.

Some of us are good at all of the above, or we think you are good at it. Church leaders can be semi-professionals at that – to be unknown or partially known, and accepted, and loved after a fashion. Well, that's what we settle for.

AND THEN THERE'S JESUS

How about this? . . . To be fully known, everything, no secrets.

You are already resisting that idea.

The good, the bad, the ugly, the shocking – to have somebody see it all, see right through you and then say to you, "I love you so much. I delight in you. I accept you. I forgive you. Let's get going. We have a lot to do together, because the crowds are in need of us."

What would it be like to have someone say:

- "I know all about you."
- "You think you are hiding, but I see you."
- "I see all of you. I see into every part of you."

- "You think that if I really saw you and knew you, I wouldn't want you. But you're wrong."

"You are wrong, because it is not about you. It's about Me and the mercy and the grace that I have to shower upon you. It's all about Me, and that's good news for you."

BLESSED

Blessed are the failures. Blessed are the empty successes. Blessed are the broken and desperate sinners. Blessed are those who need God and know it and say it.

They get the kingdom. They are *in* the kingdom. It doesn't go to anybody else. How blessed, how favored, how divinely advantaged they are!

PRESENT TENSE

And if you failed to notice, such people are blessed *now*. It is not "Blessed will be" or "Blessed should be". It is "Blessed *are* . . .." Life is now. The kingdom is now. Blessedness begins now.

CONNECTING A DOT

There's a famous invitation Jesus extends at the end of chapter 11 of Matthew's Gospel. It goes like this:

28 'Come to me, all you that are weary and are carrying heavy burdens, and I will give you rest. [29]*Take my yoke upon you and learn from me; for I am gentle and humble in heart, and you will find rest for your souls.* [30]*For my yoke is easy, and my burden is light.'*

Matthew 11:28-30

This is another one of those places I used to think "Gentle Jesus" was making a special pitch to a distinct group of people. And, well, he was, but not in the way I thought of it.

I thought Jesus was breaking from his train of thought and saying, "Okay, now I would like to take a moment and say a special word to those of you who are particularly tired, those who are weary. Yes, I have something to say to you, as well. You can come to me, too. I'll give you what you need like I do with all the others."

I totally missed it.

This is not an invitation to the severely fatigued among us.

It is, instead, a call to the only ones who would ever care to respond, the only ones who would ever hear Jesus in the first place. Jesus is speaking to the only ones who ever do come to him.

The weary, those carrying "heavy burdens" are identical with "the poor in spirit." They get the kingdom – rest for their souls, yoked with Jesus for life and ministry. And they get it now. No one else does. No one.

Matthew 11:28-30 is simply another version of the first Beatitude, the first announcement of blessing. *'Blessed are the poor in spirit, for theirs is the kingdom of heaven.'*

THE ALREADY-AND-NOT-YET BLESSEDNESS

We get the Kingdom of Heaven? When? Now. Everything we see in Jesus is ours now. What he displays of the kingdom belongs to those who come to him. Now.

And then there is a "not yet" quality to it. This kingdom will come in its fullness one day in the future. When God wraps up the whole story and ushers in a new heaven and a new earth, the kingdom will be revealed to us fully. And we will be in it. It will be his and it will be ours.

THIS TOOK LONGER

The first Beatitude is like the first Commandment of the Ten. It is first for a reason. If you don't get the first one down, you won't get the rest of them. Everything that follows builds on the first. If the first one falls, the rest go tumbling. It's a domino effect. Without the first Beatitude you can just forget about the whole thing.

The Sermon on the Mount is the foundation for life and ministry with Jesus. He'll say as much at the end (Matthew 7:24-27).

The Beatitudes are the foundation of the foundation.

The first Beatitude is the foundation of the foundation of the foundation.

It takes as long to build the foundation as it does the rest of the house. Without the foundation, the house won't stand.

Now we can get on with the rest of what Jesus has to say.

2

BLESSED: COMFORTED SORROWFUL ONES

[4]'Blessed are those who mourn,

for they will be comforted.'

Matthew 5:4

HOW IT FOLLOWS

When you begin with Jesus, or begin again with Jesus, you bring to him your spiritually bankrupt self. You bring the mess you call "me."

Then you mourn over it all.

Yes, you are a recipient of the Kingdom of Heaven, but that incredible news compels you even more to weep over your broken life with a genuine sorrow and holy regret for all that has been squandered and wasted. This is deep "repentance."

Repentance – that is to say, a change of thinking that leads to a change in life. It is a turning away from all that is empty, in order to turn toward all that is full and good, all that God is giving you.

You see your life differently now. Often the tears just come.

NOW IT IS NECESSARY

Mourning is an admission. Mourning is reflection. It is the next step and an ongoing practice in a life commitment to truth and honesty before God.

Forget about your natural gifts, strengths and skills for a minute. How's all that working for you? They aren't going to get you anywhere in the end. In fact, your reliance upon all that, the misuse of all that may be responsible for the dead end you're in.

You bring nothing of your own to God but your failure, your sin, your guilt, your shame, your emptiness. That is all you can truly call your own.

And that is the spiritual raw material God wants to work with.

Your financial hole, your failed schemes, your aborted education, your rocky marriage, your wrecked marriage, your failure as a parent, your failure in relationships, your addictions, your secret life, your emotional wounds, your chronic illness, your problems and your disappointments, all the pain you have inflicted upon others – we could go on . . .

None of these disqualify you from God's blessing. In fact, it is just the opposite. These things make you a prime candidate for God's blessing! That is, if you face them, if you acknowledge them, if you confess them and they break your pride.

"Those who mourn" are the only people who receive life and get God and all that God has for them. Nobody else does.

Name it for what it is and grieve over it. Let yourself feel the pain and weep.

Don't avoid your sorrow. Don't be afraid of your sorrow. If you haven't cried, then perhaps you haven't come to terms with your life. Maybe you're not yet ready for God.

WHAT YOU CAN MISS

Turn this second Beatitude into negatives: "Not blessed are those who do not mourn, for they shall not be comforted."

If you don't find yourself mourning the emptiness and all the damage done, you probably are not owning your own spiritual need. Back to square one. (Actually, life with Jesus is a continual return to square one, the first Beatitude. This will become clear later.)

Let's freely paraphrase a bit. Jesus is saying: *"If you want to be with me, face your garbage. Let yourself feel it as you face it. You won't be comforted, you won't be free, you won't advance with me until you do."*

SORRY FOR HIMSELF

When did you miss being comforted because you refused to mourn? It is possible to be sad and feel sorrow, to grieve and not be comforted, to grieve and not be blessed.

I testified in a military court-martial once. I was pastoring a church on the West Coast. We were located two blocks from a deep-water harbor and a U.S. Navy base.

The court martial involved a Navy chaplain. He happened to be ordained in my denomination. He was accused and then convicted of sleeping with at least one female sailor. The allegation was that he manipulated her, abused his position as counselor and spiritual shepherd, then bedded her.

I didn't know the man but was called in as an "expert witness" of sorts. I was the closest representative of his religious affiliation. I was asked questions. What were our moral standards? What were the consequences of his alleged actions within our church community? What would disciplining such a leader look like in our community?

He was drummed out of the Navy and later stripped of his ordination.

I was not present when the Navy judge gave his decision. A colleague of mine was. He had monitored the case each day and observed the chaplain on the day of judgement.

He said of the chaplain, "He was sorry for himself, but not for the young woman or for what he did." He was just sorry for himself.

It is possible to be sad and feel sorrow, to grieve and yet not "mourn" in the spirit of Jesus' words. It is possible not to be blessed in that... not to be comforted.

Are you so wrapped up in yourself, so full of denial for whatever reason, only caring about what it all means for you and not for others? You have yet to meet God.

HOW WOULD GOD COMFORT THOSE WHO MOURN?

When the scales fall from your eyes, you see all the emptiness for what it is. You also see all the collateral damage. At the same time, you begin to see all that God is and all God has for you. You see all you've been missing, all that is available ...

This would include:

- forgiveness
- acceptance
- friendship with the person of Jesus
- apprenticeship with Jesus
- like-minded companions for the journey
- life, hope, meaning and purpose

- belonging

If that's not comforting, I don't know what is.

And there's more.

You take on a genuine posture of mourning. You bring that to the table when you sit down with God. Then God says, "Bless you! I've been waiting. I have plans for you. I want you to partner with me. I want to give you a share in my ministry."

That's even more comforting.

In fact – and listen to this – out of your deepest wound you will one day minister with great power. Out of your greatest failure, where you are most broken and barren, out of that place will come life and blessing for others.

That would be an unexpected, unimaginable comfort.

You are fertile ground for the harvest God wants to reap. It's a harvest not only in your own life but also through your life to the people around you.

And the reason this is possible, the reason that you are blessed in this broken condition has nothing to do with you. The source of your blessed status has nothing to do with merit or justice or social position or achievement or the luck of the draw. Remember?

The foundation of God's world and your place in it is the mercy of God and the grace of God poured out upon your life.

That's a comfort worth waking up to every morning.

REDEEMING WHAT WAS VIOLATED

God certainly comforts those who are victims. God embraces our pain and uses it. God takes what has been done to us and how it has left us and promises to redeem it. God can make it a place of flourishing life and ministry.

Some of us are victims of terrible abuse in our lives. And some of us have then acted out our pain upon others, making them victims, as well. Isn't that right?

And some of us have secrets that we have never told anybody else. We carry all of that with us. It's all like a great weight.

All of us have made poor choices. All of us have character flaws. We have regrets and a past. All of us have a story.

THE THIRD QUESTION

These may apply here:

- What happened?
- How did it hurt you?

Those who have been victims of abuse are helped by sitting with and reflecting upon these questions, and then answering them. It's good to be clear about what you have to work with.

Jesus and his people want to meet you there.

But there is a third question that probes a critical aspect of our wounding:

- What was your sinful response?

What have been your sinful responses to hurts in your life? What unprocessed suffering in you brought out the worst in you? What do you need to identify, own, confess, and mourn over in the presence of God? If you miss this step, it will keep you bound to an unredeemed past.

We're talking here about conviction of sin. That is to say, an inner awareness of a wrong you committed.

And let's be clear. This is not something you did before you were victimized, thus suggesting the wrong done to you was somehow justified. No, this is your sinful response to the wrong done to you. If that is the case, you had a choice.

It won't let go of you until you own it. It won't let go until you give voice to it. It won't let go until with regret you say you are sorry for it in the presence of God.

Sure, everyone is a victim in varying degrees and from time to time. But it is equally true that when hurt we tend to hurt back, responding in the same spirit. If we're honest, this is a steady presence and reality in our lives and in our choices.

That impulse doesn't help you. You're just further hurting yourself.

You can be freed of that.

HOW THIS FOLLOWS

Jesus is saying to his followers:

"Listen, if you want to be with me, if you want a share in what I am doing, if you want to do the things that I am doing, don't run away from your own story. Don't avoid reflection and sorrow over your past – whether things were done to you, or you did things to other people or some combination.

"Don't sidestep your grief, your remorse, your holy regret, your sorrowful admission over all that was not of God. Turn around and look at me and then yourself. God will exchange his beauty for your ashes." (Isaiah 61:1-4; Luke 4:16-21)

That's a comfort.

Jesus again, in so many words – "Don't fill up your life with busyness, so you don't have to face the sadness. Let it come! There is great blessing in it. God will comfort you! This is part of being my disciple; this is part of having your share in my kingdom.

"You don't get there any other way except in this way and on this road. You will get nowhere with me, if you don't do this. Trust me."

3

BLESSED: ALL-INHERITING HUMBLE ONES

5 'Blessed are the meek,
for they will inherit the earth.'

Matthew 5:5

EVERYBODY WANTS IT

As I write:

- China continues to build artificial islands with anchorages and airstrips in the South China Sea. This is in dispute with Vietnam, the Philippines and Malaysia.

- The Russians now occupy 20% of the nation of Georgia, control the annexed Crimean Peninsula (2014), would love all of Ukraine, and have firmly re-established themselves in the Middle East.

- The territorial presence of ISIS as a physical caliphate in Iraq and Syria is gone. But the organization is spreading throughout the world, as is Al Qaeda and affiliates.

- Iran finally has her long-desired control in Iraq with its Shi'ite majority. The goal is for similar influence in Syria which would offer an open lane for her to the Mediterranean Sea.

I could go on and on, because the list goes on and on.

Bottom line, everybody wants more and more of the planet. That would include us – the good ole USA.

The 20th century is not called "the American century" for nothing. It began with President Teddy Roosevelt sending sixteen (count 'em) of our new battleships with their hulls painted white – thus called the Great White Fleet – on a two-year world tour. We were announcing American strength and helping secure our growing overseas interests and holdings.

Everybody always wants and is constantly striving for a bigger and bigger piece of the pie. Everybody wants to rule the world, to control the world in one way or another. It's always been this way and always will be this way . . . until God brings the whole story to a close.

Everybody is striving and maneuvering and conniving to make the earth theirs – except for "the meek"! Without lifting a finger, they are going to inherit the whole thing. That is, if Jesus knew what he was talking about.

REPEATING HOW WE GOT HERE

Jesus sits down with his followers and says in so many words,

"If you really want to be with me, have a share in what I am doing and do the things I am doing, you've got to change the way you think. You've got to change how you see things, what you believe about the world and how it operates."

First things first, the foundation of the world and you're standing in it is not based on justice. It is not based on merit. It is not based on some kind of inherited privilege, nor is it based on the luck of the draw. The foundation of the world and you're standing in it is based on the mercy of God and the grace of God poured out upon your life. Period.

That's a long way of saying *"Blessed are the poor in spirit, for theirs is the kingdom of heaven"* . . . and no one else's.

You come to God with nothing. God says to you in your broken pride, "I'll take your nothing and give you everything. Welcome to life with me in my kingdom. It now belongs to you." That is Blessing #1.

And Blessing #2 follows from and goes hand in hand with that broken pride of yours. Blessing #2 is then a genuine sorrow and regret over the wreckage of your life. It is a deep reflection and remorse over it all and over all those affected by it. *"Blessed are those who mourn, for they shall be comforted."*

"Mourning" is a renouncing and a refusal. Resorting to the ways of the world has had its day. You used to cling to and operate by them. It was all a big lie. That's going away. And God comforts you.

THESE STATEMENTS BUILD ON ONE ANOTHER

Jesus' third announcement of blessing is not so much what you do next. Instead, the third Beatitude is what the first two Beatitudes lead to. The third Beatitude is about what the first two produce, what issues out of spiritual bankruptcy and genuine mourning when we give all that to God.

All to say, the third Beatitude announces a change inside of us. We experience a shift in our character. We find within us the formation of "meekness."

MEEK IS NOT WEAK

That was not my goal when I was a kid – to grow up and be a meek person. I wanted that in no way, shape or form. Meek was not a positive word in my vocabulary. I would have associated "meek" with "weak" and other words beginning with a "w," like "wimp" and "wussy."

What does Jesus mean by "meek" here?

Well for one thing, he does not mean weak. "Meek" is not "weak."

"Meek" and "meekness" here are, on the contrary, a kind of strength. "Meek" is not necessarily physical strength, although it can often include that. "Meek" always and by definition is, rather, an inner firmness.

Meekness is an inner power that typically does not assert itself, does not need to assert itself. It is a confident resolve that is restrained, not knee-jerk reactive, not out-of-control responsive.

Meekness is in-control responsive. It is self-controlled, yourself under control, submitted and surrendered to God's control.

Meekness is humility.

As a shift in character, you do not go after it. You do not seize it. Meekness, humility is given to you. It is formed within you. It is born out of your broken pride, poverty of spirit and mourning over your life.

To be meek is to come to a true estimate of yourself and of God. Who said that? The Jesuits? (Seems like I jotted it down as a note at some point.) Regardless, it sums up and captures what is at stake.

What is at stake is living in the freedom of the knowledge of two realities: 1) who you are in all your limitations; and 2) who the limitless God is within you and in the world around you.

If in your deep heart you embrace the previous paragraph and put your trust in that, something remarkable happens. You are released from the neurotic drive to lay hold of and control everything around you.

You don't have to relate to everything and everyone with manipulation, coercion or violence anymore. You are free of that. No more fear.

Meekness means having the capacity for battle but battle on your terms. Not trading blow for blow. Not some worldly power struggle, but, instead, taking the blows and absorbing the violence into yourself. You smother evil. You take away all its oxygen. Darkness doesn't know what to do with that.

When you think of it all in those terms, meekness as strength makes sense. As someone mentioned to me recently, "You think meek is weak? Try being meek for a week!"

SOME OF THE MEEK AMONG US

To whom can we point as an illustration of meek?

They say Abraham Lincoln was meek. Quiet in his spirit, not wanting war, and then absorbing so much of the war he oversaw into himself. If you follow successive photographs of him in the 1860's, you can see it in his changing face.

People say Rosa Parks was meek in a way. She didn't attack. She simply refused to get up and go to the back of the bus, come what may.

Her friend, Martin Luther King, enjoyed the same reputation. A man of tremendous influence. Not a man of violence. Humble. In other words, meek.

None of them were perfect by any stretch, but all of them leaders, all of them strong, all of them victorious. All of them meek.

And, of course, Jesus was meek. He says so himself. Here's that passage again . . .

[28] *"Come to me, all you that are weary and are carrying heavy burdens, and I will give you rest.* [29]*Take my yoke upon you, and learn from me; for I am gentle and* ***humble*** *in heart,* (the Greek word here is the same as in our Beatitude) . . . *for I am gentle and meek in heart and you will find rest for your souls."*

Matthew 11:28-29

When describing Jesus' "triumphal entry" into Jerusalem, Matthew 21:5 quotes Zechariah 9:9 which puts it this way . . .

"Tell the daughter of Zion, Look, your king is coming to you, ***humble*** (same word again, also translated "meek") . . . *meek and mounted on a donkey, . . .'*

Meek is Jesus, and meek is not weak.

How does one become meek? Again, it is a gift of true mourning. It comes through suffering and sorrow. It comes from the death of the old self – not resisting that death but entering into it and responding to it well. Meekness is given.*

---

*For a penetrating journey from self-assurance through mourning and then the formation of meekness, follow the character transformation of Elizabeth and Mr. Darcy in Jane Austin's *Pride and Prejudice*.

Dietrich Bonhoeffer, a powerfully "meek" German pastor and martyr who was hung by the Nazis in 1945 sums it up best:

> To the powerless and disenfranchised, the very earth belongs. Those who now possess it by violence and injustice shall lose it. And those who have utterly renounced it, who are meek to the point of the cross, shall rule it – a new earth.
>
> from *The Cost of Discipleship.*
> (Touchstone: New York, 1995), p. 110

WHEN DO THEY INHERIT?

Now the followers of Jesus walk freely in what will one day be theirs. Now the supposedly strong who have the temporary title papers oppress the meek who know it is theirs. Now the meek are strong in patience which is nothing less than faith, hope and love.

As in any inheritance, it is an already-but-not-yet reality.

Later, at the end of history as we know it, the One who uttered these Beatitude words and who has all authority in heaven and on earth will hand over the latter to his people. That ending will be a beginning.

4

BLESSED: RIGHTEOUSNESS-DESIRING FILLED ONES

[6]"Blessed are those who hunger and thirst for righteousness, for they will be filled.'

Matthew 5:6

A CHANGE IN DIET

As the people of God – that is, Jesus' people – are transformed in their hearts and minds they grow an appetite. They are poor in spirit, mourning over their life and made increasingly meek by it all. Their desires shift in line with their changing character.

Meekness wants something else in life. Humility hungers for something different than before. Something different from the old life, the former life, the false life.

In that old life people were malnourished. Satiated on spiritual junk food, they had the sense of being full while starving to death.

Now the people of God hunger for what is true and lasting and good. They find themselves famished. They are starving for one thing.

They want "righteousness."

They hunger and thirst for it.

WHAT DOES IT MEAN?

What does it mean to hunger and thirst for righteousness?

It means that people have a craving. People are starving . . . for God. Nothing else can now satisfy. They want God, and then they want more and more of God. They want God, the ways of God and the will of God. They want "the will of God, nothing more, nothing less, nothing else."*

They want Life with a capital "L". Life with God and Life with each other according to the ways of God and the will of God.

They pray accordingly, "Your kingdom come, your will be done on earth as in heaven," found later in the Sermon on the Mount.

Jesus calls this "righteousness." Keep reading the Sermon on the Mount and Jesus will spell it out for you again and again and again.

And Jesus' people will get their fill of what they want. That's the promise and the blessing attached to this hungering and thirsting condition. Their appetite shall be satisfied.

WHAT IS IT LIKE?

Most of us have memories related to some degree of hunger and thirst. Many of mine have to do with physical exertion –not from hard labor per se – but from recreation.

Some years ago, I took a bike trip through the Canadian Rockies – from the city of Jasper to Calgary, Alberta. The first day we rode 100 miles up past a glacier along the "Ice Fields Park Way," arriving late afternoon at Lake Louise. That evening we sat down at a restaurant. I ordered dinner and ate it. Then I ordered again, another full dinner. I ate that one, too. We were hungry.

But I have never been hungry like some of you reading this.

---

*I love that phrasing, found in *Discerning God's Will Together* by Danny Morris and Charles Olsen (Nashville: Upper Room Books, 1997, p. 90) quoted in *Pursuing God's Will Together* by Ruth Haley Barton (Downers Grove: InterVarsity Press, 2012, p. 63).

Some of you have grown up in poverty, whether here in the USA or in another country. Perhaps you have a memory of a hunger that was lingering and would last for days and weeks. Maybe you had enough food to take the edge off it, but it wasn't enough to eliminate it. You were always thinking, "I wish I had more to eat."

Or maybe you've had a hospital thirst. You came out of a surgery that initially did not allow you to drink water. They gave you little ice chips to suck on. That took the edge off, but it didn't quench the dominating desire for water.

Here Jesus is talking about a hospital-like thirst, a poverty-level-like hunger that just gnaws at you. It says, "Pay attention to me. I am not going away." You must reckon with it. It is serious. The hunger and thirst must be satisfied.

LIKE THE STREAM

And then there's that well-known story in C.S. Lewis's "The Chronicles of Narnia," Book 4 (*The Silver Chair*). It's about a thirsty little girl named Jill.

If you are not familiar with the series, the first book introduces us to the world of Narnia and some of the characters, including Jill. She is one of four English school children who have stepped into Narnia through a secret, porous-like back wall of a wardrobe, taking them into another dimension.

Back in Narnia in Book 4, Jill gets separated from the rest of the children. She is lost. She is in a forest. She is gripped with a desperate, serious thirst.

She comes to a clearing. She looks out into the clearing and sees a full and flowing stream running through the middle of the clearing. The only problem is there's a huge lion sitting next to the stream. And, of course, this is Aslan, the Christ figure in the Narnia stories.

The lion spots Jill and starts talking to her in clipped, one-liners. "If you are thirsty, you may drink."

Jill, of course, is afraid of this lion, especially a lion that talks.

She begins to ask questions. She suggests that he might take a break, go away while she refreshes herself. The story says the Lion responds "with a look and a very low growl." Not too happy about that.

"Do you eat girls," she asks?

"I have eaten men and women, boys and girls, kings and kingdoms." No comfort there.

Jill continues voicing her anxiety as she inches her way beyond the tree line and out into the open towards the stream. But she dares not get near the lion.

She decides out loud, "I suppose I must go and look for another stream."

"There is no other stream," says the Lion.

Her thirst becomes more powerful than her fear.

Jill then makes the gravest decision she has ever made in her life. She moves to the stream, kneels down in front of the Lion, and begins to take in great drafts of water. The storyteller then says, "It was like no water she ever had, because it quenched your thirst at once."

And the truth is, if you want water from that stream – and by the way, there is, indeed, "no other stream" just as the Lion tells Jill – you've got to come close to the Lion. You've got to get right next to the Lion.

That's Lewis version of what Jesus is describing in this Beatitude. [6]*'Blessed are those who hunger and thirst for righteousness, for they will be filled.'*

SATISFACTION

This reminds me of my Turkish friend, Leyla (pronounced LAY-la). Now married and with a child, Leyla was a thoroughly secularized student in a Turkish university in the late 1990's.

One day she wandered into a hole-in-the-wall, secondhand book shop. The proprietor, an elderly, retired businessman (more about him in the next chapter) was standing behind the counter. Leyla looked about and began browsing. All the religious books were together on an old set of semi-dusty shelves behind the man. Only he could reach them.

Leyla spied what appeared to be a single New Testament. It was the only new book among the bunch. It said *Incil* (pronounced EEN-jeel which is Turkish for "gospel") on the spine. Otherwise, she wouldn't have known.

She had never actually seen one of these before, let alone read anything in it. She had just heard about them along with all the negative nonsense said about them in Turkish public education, designed to sway children and youth away.

Leyla asked to look at it. The man obliged her. Such a shiny new book had to be expensive, beyond her limited funds. She asked, "How much?

It was literally pennies. She thought, "I must be looking quite broke!"

She bought it.

As Leyla was leaving with it and just at the door, the man called after her. "Young lady, after you read some of that, I'd like for you to come back and let me know what you think of it."

Leyla went home, opened it up, and stayed up much of the night reading the stories about Jesus. Her hunger for truth was fighting against other feelings within. As she puts it, she had "programmed [myself] not to believe in the *Incil* and just criticize it as a feminist, humanist and a socialist young woman so that [I could] feel free to become an atheist and get rid of religion." She underlined things she liked or had questions about. She found herself weeping as she read.

Leyla had never encountered anything like it. Had never been presented with a person like Jesus in her life. Sort of like Jill lapping up the water from the stream.

She began visiting the old man, almost every day after classes. He listened and answered her questions with patience and love. They stopped their conversations whenever a customer entered the shop. It was dangerous to talk openly about Christianity.

The parable of the seed, the sower and the four soils (Gospel of Mark, chapter 4) finally broke Leyla open. As she puts it, her "heart was coming alive and connecting with a source that was full of peace and joy." She asked God to make her heart good soil for the seeds planted from her reading.

Leyla shared with her elderly friend what was happening within her. He in turn explained to her further what was happening within her. He shared the gospel message with her and led her in a prayer. Leyla gave her heart, mind, body and soul to the One she had been hungering and thirsting for.

6 *'Blessed are those who hunger and thirst for righteousness, for they will be filled.'*

THE ONLY THING

Jesus is speaking of the "God-shaped vacuum" residing within each person. You may have heard people refer to this. We trace the image back to Blaise Pascal in the early 17th century.

> *What else does this craving, and this helplessness, proclaim but that there was once in man a true happiness, of which all that now remains is the empty print and trace? This he tries in vain to fill with everything around him, seeking in things that are not there the help he cannot find in those that are, though none can help, since this infinite abyss can be filled only with an infinite and immutable object: in other words by God himself.*
>
> - Blaise Pascal, *Pensées VIII* (425)

We've already said it. Jesus puts a name to it. It is righteousness we want, the ways of God and the will of God. What we want is God.

And only the humble, only the meek, only those who are undergoing a shift in their character by the mercy and grace of God have an appetite for God. The all-possessing empty ones, becoming the comforted sorrowful ones, becoming the all-inheriting humble ones, become the righteousness-desiring filled ones.

And the blessing, the promise is that God will give you what you want. Filled to the brim and then some. But now we're getting ahead of ourselves again.

A QUESTION

As you are reading this, what are you hungering and thirsting for?

What have you identified as the object of your famished craving for satisfaction?

A close friend? A set of friends? A life-partner? Career success? Public recognition? Non-stop fun and pleasure? Making everybody happy all the time? Affirmation. Freedom from the shame that binds you? Forgiveness? Making everything right in every situation, bringing the solution to every problem? A vision for your local church?* Money and security? Power? Being known as a champion of the poor and oppressed? Being a perfect little person? The list is even longer . . .

Not one of those things is going to satisfy the hunger and thirst within you. Not one of those things can fill that vacuum, that God-shaped vacuum within you.

Only God can. And God will.

---

*In *Life Together* Dietrich Bonhoeffer called this a "dream-wish," and insisted God hates that kind of thing due to its destructive fruit. But that's for another book and another time.

HERE'S SOME MORE GOOD NEWS

This invitation is not for righteous people. Jesus does not say, "Blessed are the righteous, the people who know God and have attained some kind of obedient life or are striving for that." He will, however, say that in time.

Now he simply says, "Blessed are those who *want* righteousness, who want God and the ways of God and the will of God. God bless those people. God bless you! You will get your fill . . . ."

But you won't fill yourselves. God will fill you. God will satisfy you.

St. Augustine said in the 5th century something like "The will to be righteous is a large part of righteousness." Jesus says here that a hunger and thirst for righteousness is the key to it.

INTERLUDE

LIKE AN ASCENDING SPIRAL

Did you catch this statement a page or two ago?

> The all-possessing empty ones, becoming the comforted sorrowful ones, becoming the all-inheriting humble ones, become the righteousness-desiring filled ones.

These statements of blessing progress from one to the next. One gives birth to the next. They build on one another, but not in a straight line. Rather, they move in something like a widening, ascending spiral.

We keep coming back around to being "poor in spirit." As our awareness of our own sin deepens, we return to "square one." And yet we are still in the kingdom, but now "further up and further in" as C.S. Lewis once put it.

And as we ascend, all the features of the blessed life expand in scope, increasing in their power and effect.

Greater awareness, deeper repentance, increased humility and greater spiritual hunger and filling. More and more freedom. This will all become clearer as we proceed.

IT'S A STORY

Yes, the Beatitudes are connected and build on one another. And they will continue to unfold, one after another as we proceed in the following chapters.

But at this point stop and consider what you are seeing. You are tracing the transformation of a human life. You are watching a broken person turn into a whole and healthy and fulfilled person.

Again, Jesus' Beatitudes are not disconnected proverbial statements. These are not "pearls of wisdom" randomly strung together. Instead, they form a progression, a step-by-step movement, an account of how people can actually change.

The Beatitudes are a story. That's right, a story. And the story is true. And the story has been and continues to be repeated down through the ages to this present day and beyond.

As the old gospel song puts it:

> *It is no secret what God can do.*
> *What he has done for others, He'll do for you.*

Jesus is telling a story.

It can be your story.

And there's more. This story now turns the world upside down.

5

BLESSED: EVER-RECEIVING MERCY GIVERS

[7]'Blessed are the merciful,

for they will receive mercy.'

Matthew 5:7

WE KEEP SAYING IT, BECAUSE YOU NEED TO KEEP HEARING IT

That meekness, that humility taking shape in you has an appetite. It hungers for things of value, things that last. It wants God and the ways of God and the will of God. It wants life with a capital "L." You get filled up with what you want. Jesus calls it "righteousness."

You get showered with all this generous, almost reckless giving by God. And this is all to say what we believe Jesus to be saying with each line: the foundation of the world and your standing in it is based *not* on justice, not on merit, not on some kind of inherited privilege, not on the luck of the draw.

The foundation of the world and your standing in it is based on the mercy of God and the grace of God poured out upon your life.

Mercy. That powerful word takes us into Jesus' next statement of blessing.

Again, [7]*'Blessed are the merciful, for they will receive mercy.'*

ALL THAT IS GIVEN STARTS GIVING

Mercy is the reaction, the after effect, the consequence of being filled with righteousness. Mercy is the face of righteousness. Mercy is the "front man," the lead singer.

Being merciful is the immediate outflow. Extending mercy is the overflow of righteousness, brimming up inside you, spilling out of you, and getting all over the people around you.

DEFINITIONS

Let's back up and ask a question: What exactly is mercy?

Mercy is simply this: *not* getting what you *do* deserve.

Let's say that again.

Mercy is *not* getting what you *do* deserve . . . what you *do* deserve being some form of judgment, some form of painful payback in the name of justice which is rightfully due you. *Not* getting what you *do* deserve. That's mercy.

Grace, on the other hand, is *getting* what you *don't* deserve. That would be a gift you have not earned, not merited per se – given out of sheer generosity, largesse, and the freedom of another.

Neither mercy nor grace are based on something in the recipient. Neither one is a payment due, making good on some claim, fulfilling an obligation. They are not dependent on anything in or about the recipient. Both mercy and grace are based on something completely within the giver.

A STORY OF MERCY

When you are young you do stupid things. When you are old you do stupid things. I was young, in graduate school in southern California, in my more serious cycling days – as in bicycle (road/racing bike, not a mountain bike.)

One particular morning I was out with my atheist, Canadian cycling partner, also a graduate student. Let's call him Richard. We were exploring the upper reaches of a Los Angeles County park in the San Gabriel Mountains. It was time to head home.

Gravity did all the work. Early a.m., no one around. Way beyond the speed limit, blasting through several stop signs all the way down to where it dumped us out onto old Route 66. We crossed traffic and then headed east, again, without ever stopping.

What we didn't know was that an LA County Deputy Sheriff was right behind us the entire time.

The siren blips, the lights go on.

We pull off onto the dirt shoulder and get off our bikes. He pulls up and steps out of his cruiser.

"Are you guys aware that you were going [such and such] miles an hour, ran three stop signs, then didn't look or stop as you turned onto Foothill Blvd?"

What were we going to say? We actually weren't paying much attention, maybe half attention. I forget what we said.

He pulls out his ticket book. Now they use a handheld, wireless device connected to the courthouse.

(There's another piece to this. It was just the previous week, that I had graduated traffic school for speeding in my car!)

"Officer," I said, "will this ticket go on my driving record?" He responded, "Yeah, it will." Inner panic. Skyrocketing insurance premiums, diving deeper into graduate student poverty, etc.

I then said, slowly and deliberately, "Wait. Before you do anything, I'd like to ask for your mercy." (I used the "m" word. Remember, "mercy" equals not getting what you do deserve.) I followed with, "We are very sorry for our actions. If we promise never to do this again, would you not write the ticket?"

The officer paused, surveyed me and then Richard. He said nothing. It was as if he had never heard the "m" word before. People admitting guilt? Sure. Apologizing? Yes. (We just had.) Asking for a break? All the time. But appealing to something different in him, to mercy? By the look on his face that apparently came as a new one.

He looked at our bikes. He thought some more. Then he asked, "What kind of bikes are those?" We showed him, talked about the bikes. He talked about *his* bike.

Then he paused, reflected more and said, "You guys be careful now. Have a good day."

With that he put his ticket book away, got in his car, and drove off. We watched as he blended into the traffic.

Richard looked at me in wonder, and said heavily and slowly, "H o w did y o u d o *that*?"

I didn't do *that*. The officer did that. It was nothing in me. It was something in him, that flowed out of him. And it wasn't grace, it was mercy. Not getting what we did deserve.

ANOTHER STORY

And then this came around the same time as the bike incident. I heard it from a Presbyterian minister as he was speaking one Sunday evening in his church in Edinburgh, Scotland.

The pastor was in his early 70's, about to retire. He was teaching from the Old Testament book of the Prophet Amos.

I forget the exact connection to Amos, but at one point he shared of being a young officer in the British army in his early 20's. It was World War II. He saw heavy action in Burma and Thailand.

On patrol one day in the jungle he and his unit were ambushed by local guerilla fighters in league with the Japanese. They took casualties. The carnage was terrible. The patrol beat back the attackers and sent them running.

Our storyteller found himself with his foot on the neck of an enemy fighter, face up on the ground. The young officer had his gun pointed and ready to pull the trigger. The impulse was to shoot.

But something within him came out of him at that critical moment. He remembered thinking to himself as he looked into the man's terrified eyes, "No, I'm going to let you live."

And then this sentence came into his mind, "So this is what mercy is."

He never forgot that moment.

Mercy – not getting what you do deserve.

AND YET ANOTHER STORY

In the previous chapter you'll recall the older Turkish gentleman who sold a New Testament to my friend, Leyla.

Sometime after he told her the gospel story, and she embraced it, he told her his story. Leyla recounted it to me.

The man had actually been a wealthy businessperson and an atheist much of his life, not even a nominal Muslim . . . more of a nothing. As he was in his early 60's he was looking at a comfortable retirement and a life of ease. Then he was diagnosed with inoperable, untreatable cancer.

He has money, so he heads to Beirut, Lebanon for a second opinion. Same conclusion. He flies to Europe, seeking further opinions and the best treatment money can buy. Same answer. No hope – inoperable, untreatable.

He returns to Turkey. He's lying in bed one night, sleepless. His wife is asleep next to him and was not awakened by what happened next.

He sits up in bed. He is at the end of his resources, the end of his options. He's an atheist, mind you, but cries out in desperation, "God, save me!"

A bright light fills the room. A figure, a silhouette appears before him at the end of the bed. He has had no experience of Jesus before. No knowledge of Jesus apart from cultural, Islamic understandings of him as a prophet and then some marginal, rejected, Christian notions of Jesus.

As he beholds the apparition, he knows who it is. And then it speaks, that is, Jesus speaks. This is all he says, "Alright, I'll save you, but you're going to have to follow me."

That was it. (And, by the way, all this was in Turkish, of course Jesus knows Turkish too.)

The light and the figure lingered for a bit. The man was transfixed. Wouldn't you be? Then it all gradually faded. The room returned to the dark of night. He laid himself back down.

Eventually he fell back to sleep.

Within days he was back with his cancer doctor for a check-up. Results? All of it, gone. All gone. One of those.

He becomes a follower of Jesus. He gets to know the Christian scriptures. He retires. Opens up his little hole-in-the-wall bookshop, always with a single Turkish New Testament on the dusty shelves behind the counter. Ready when Leyla and who knows how many other lost and troubled students before and after her wandered in.

That is mercy. One who has rejected God, not getting what he does deserve – which is judgement. And then grace, getting what he doesn't deserve – forgiveness, a healed body and a purpose beyond himself.

Had nothing to do with him. Had everything to do with God.

God is so good. God is so beautiful.

Mercy is the outflow, the expression of righteousness-filled people and of a righteous God who loves to dispense it – liberally, generously, recklessly.

WHAT IS YOUR MERCY STORY?

Let me tell you your mercy story. You stand before the heavenly Judge with more than enough evidence to convict, deserving justice, and he says: "Guilty, but pardoned. Another has taken your place; another has taken your penalty, paying the price for you at the hands of Roman executioners on a lonely cross long ago. You have received mercy and now grace, as well. You are forgiven."

That's better than what a Los Angeles County Deputy Sheriff could ever offer. That's better than what a young soldier could deliver to a violent captive. That's even more than a miraculous, physical healing.

So how can you hold things against one another anymore? How can you withhold mercy from each other?

But let's not turn this into a "should." Here it does not appear as a command. Jesus is nowhere making demands. There are no "you better," "you must," "you ought to" imperatives issued here or in any of the Beatitudes!

In the Beatitudes Jesus is describing what people look like when they begin keeping company with God.

So, I'm only speaking to those of you who are getting to know God. Righteousness is filling you. Mercy is the outflow. Who is next to receive it from you? To whom will you be extending mercy? You can't stop it. It takes on a life of its own.

ALL PART OF THE TEARDOWN

And now as an over-and-over-again blessed one, you see the ongoing effect of the wrecking ball within you. Dietrich Bonhoeffer puts it this way:

> These [people] without possessions or power, these strangers on earth, these sinners, these followers of Jesus, have in their life with him renounced their own dignity, for they are merciful. As if their own needs and their own distress were not enough, they take upon themselves the distress and humiliation and sin of others . . . In order that they may be merciful they cast away the most priceless treasure of human life, their personal dignity and honor. For the only honor and dignity they know is their Lord's own mercy, to which alone they owe their very lives.*

And, of course, as you begin to insist upon and insert mercy into the merciless world around you, you yourself become a blessed wrecking ball to the malevolent enemy – the hopeless, violent culture of death.

Mercy is a wrecking ball, breaking down what is brittle and hollow and false. Mercy is a prophetic "No!" to a merciless world. Mercy is a challenge to the system. It is a defiant confrontation. It insists on a redemptive hope for any and all.

The presence of mercy is a threat. It is a wrecking ball to the executioners among us. They won't tolerate this for long.

**The Cost of Discipleship. Touchstone: New York, 1995. p. 111.*

MORE TO COME

And we didn't even get to the part about you receiving even more mercy. You giving mercy is the sign that you have received and will receive mercy. Not something earned. Rather as a gift of grace.

Dietrich Bonhoeffer again:

> One day God himself will come down and take upon himself their sin and shame. He will cover them with his own honor and remove their disgrace. It will be his glory to bear the shame of sinners and to clothe them with his honor. Blessed are the merciful, for they have the Merciful for their Lord.*

**The Cost of Discipleship. Touchstone: New York, 1995. p. 111-112.*

6

BLESSED: WANTING-GOD-AND-SPOTTING-GOD-HEARTS

[8]'Blessed are the pure in heart,
for they will see God.'

Matthew 5:8

MORE THAN MERCY

We're hungering and thirsting for righteousness – for the ways of God and the will of God. We want nothing more, nothing less, nothing else. Wanting righteousness is a desire for God and everything God is about.

The promise is that you will be filled with that. God will do the filling. It then overflows and spills out of you, getting on everyone around you. Jesus moves into three blessed expressions of that overflow. The first comes in the form of extending mercy to those around you.

The second comes as something taking shape in you. It comes as the formation of a heart. A heart that thinks and cares only about what God thinks and cares about. Such a heart is powerful simply as it beats, let alone acts!

THE "HEART" IN THE WEST

You've heard a lot about the heart since childhood.

- "Follow your heart!"
- "The heart has its reasons."
- "Don't listen to your head, listen to your heart."
- "Have a heart."
- "My Heart Will Go On" from Titanic – Celine Dion
- "The Heart Wants What It Wants" – Selena Gomez
- "I Left My Heart in San Francisco" (This would date you as even older than a Baby Boomer.)

When Western, popular culture says "heart," it is referring to feelings, emotions, gut impulses. We are told that these are not influenced by any mental corrupting presence, not touched by an encumbered and restricted mind. We are to celebrate emotion and impulse over against a reasoning brain.

This view of the individual sees emotion and feeling as the true you. The supposed false you is associated with thinking and reflection. The false you would be the result of societal norms putting people in chains who are otherwise born free.*

"Get out of your head and into your heart!"

THE HEART IN THE BIBLE

Yes, in the Bible the "heart" is the real and true self. But that is the case only when the word is understood in broader, more encompassing terms.

Yes, the "heart" is the seat of one's emotions. But it is also the center of one's volition, intellect, and decision making. And the heart in this broader meaning is the internal sphere in which God is encountered. (See Ps 27:8; Eph 3:17.)

The heart is the home of personal feeling, thinking and willing. When the Bible says "heart," think heart, mind and will. It's all there. It is mission control, your personal guidance system, that which rules your life.

---

*So claimed Jean Jacques Rousseau and the Romantic Movement of the late 18th century through the middle of the 19th century, then coming into resurgence again in the 1960's until today.

In light of the above, it makes sense that later in Matthew Jesus says things like, "Out of the abundance of the heart the mouth speaks" (Matthew 12:34; cf. Luke 6:45). In other words, what comes out of your mouth proceeds from the essence of who you are.

What comes out of the spigot reflects the quality of what is in the well beneath it. Good well, good water flowing. Bad well, bad water flowing. The outer quality of the life is determined by the inner quality of the heart in all that it embraces – thought, feeling, decision making.

JESUS' REALISM

Jesus is not dreamy naïve about people. He gives a dose of reality in one of his many spoilers: *"Out of the heart come evil intentions – murder, adultery, fornication, theft, false witness, slander."* (Matthew 15) He falls in with a long line of prophets who were equally realistic. *"The human heart is deceitful above all things, and desperately wicked; who can know it?"* (Jeremiah 17:9)

Apart from God your heart can talk you into all kinds of spiritually toxic, stupid things. And then you do them.

Sorry to ruin the party. We come into the world as damaged goods. Unbiased observation ought to confirm that for you. G.K. Chesterton was the one who remarked in so many words that "original sin" is the only doctrine that can be empirically verified. And it certainly can be.

My office at the first church I served backed up to the play yard of the daycare and pre-school. Cute, yeah, but those little ones could get pretty mean. Sharing was not bubbling out of them. And it wasn't because a pack of self-serving parents got to them first and wrecked them. They were already like that. They were and are – we were and are – with a turned-in-on-themselves selfish orientation, albeit with exceptional, sweet moments.

Yes, Jesus is neither sentimental nor triumphalist about the human condition lodged in the heart. He has more of a tragic, realistic view of people. But he also has hope.

HOPE

Something has to happen to the heart. It needs to be purified. It can be purified.

"Purity" is another term needing some definition. "Pure of heart" is not Jesus' way of talking about unblemished, perfect little people.

Oh, sure, he *is* talking about those who are hungry for and filled up with righteousness. He *is* talking about those whose lives conform to that righteousness as they follow God. The majority of the Sermon on the Mount is devoted to fleshing that out. See the end of Matthew 5.

But this Beatitude is not zeroing in on a high bar moralism. What Jesus is talking about here is more of a life-focus for those on a journey with God.

In line with what we have been saying, this is about a life orientation. Wanting God, the ways of God and the will of God. Nothing more, nothing less, nothing else. Think single mindedness. Heart, mind and will, all committed to the same direction, to the same object, to one thing. All in. Nothing else matters. The Bible might call it an "undivided heart."

The 19th century Danish philosopher and Christian, Soren Kierkegaard, wrote a book entitled *Purity of Heart is to Will One Thing.* That's getting at what pure hearted people are about. And the "one thing" is God. What they are given makes them blessed and confirms this understanding. They are all about God, and the blessing is that they will "see" God.

HOW AND WHEN?

They will "see" God? Most readers take this as a reference to standing in God's presence at the end of time and gazing upon God to whatever extent that is possible. There is a mixed reading on this possibility in the Bible. Some say it is impossible (John 1:18; I Tim 6:15-16). Others recount an occurrence or a guarantee of it (Psalm 11:7; 17:15; Job 19:26; Rev 22:3-4).

Perhaps it is a reference to coming to recognize the Father in the person of his Son whom we have "seen" (John 1:18; 14:9; II Corinthians 5:16).

Or maybe it is something else – an increased ability to recognize the presence and activity of God in the course of everyday life. God spotters. People who can identify what God is up to, get alongside of it and cooperate with it.

Back to pure-hearted people. What would be some examples of individuals willing one thing? We're not talking Jesus-followers necessarily. Just people who seem to see only one thing. What people possessing such pure, willing-one-thing hearts come to mind?

- William Wallace (at least the Hollywood version) would be such a person. Yeah, "Braveheart." Eight hundred years ago in Scotland there was only one thing for him – freedom from the English. That was it. Even at the point of a prolonged and painful death he refused to renounce the cause.

- And then there was the Englishman, Winston Churchill. Beginning in the 1930's there was increasingly only one thing for him. Defeat Nazi Germany. Never surrender.

- Harriet Tubman and Sojourner Truth – devoting themselves completely to freeing slaves and putting an end to the institution.

- Vincent van Gogh – painting with an urgency and devotion. Never selling anything he produced, but never letting go of his brush.

- Any top performing athlete. You have to be "selfish" and say "No" to a lot of other things in order to say "Yes" to the one thing. Serena and Venus Williams, Tom Brady, Wayne Gretsky, Michael Jordan, Roger Federer.

All of these are examples and images of "pure" hearts.

Back to followers of Jesus. John McKay was the president of Princeton Seminary during the middle portion of the last century. He was known to say, "I have one passion in life, and it is Him!" That's a pure heart.

The founder of the movement that produced the Reformed and Presbyterian churches 500 years ago, John Calvin, had a personal seal.

The image was of a heart in a hand outstretched and given to the living God. That's a pure heart!

The kind of pure heart Jesus is speaking of and personally embodied ensures blessing. Those who possess the heart are blessed. And those who are around such people are blessed. They are blessed with God himself.

THE WEIGHT OF IT

But, as with the merciful, the "pure in heart" represent a rejection. They offer another prophetic "No!" to a world with a contrary heart.

This is a challenge to the system, in defiance of the way things are. The pure in heart refuse to move. They won't budge. They live in the will of

God. They want God and the ways of God. Nothing more, nothing less, nothing else.

The presence of a pure heart is a threat. It is a blessed wrecking ball to the façade of happiness and blessedness being found in a devotion to other things. A pure heart unmasks the charade and shows it for what it is.

As with the merciful, the world will not tolerate this for long.

7

BLESSED: NAMED-FOR-GOD PEACEMAKERS

[9] 'Blessed are the peacemakers,
for they will be called children of God.'

Matthew 5:9

ARE YOU KIDDING?

The world system thrives on enmity and fear. There is money to be made. There is power to be had. There is advantage to be gained in the dividing of people one from another, one tribe against another, one city over another, one nation attacking another.

Who wants peace? If we wanted peace we would forgive and try to make things right with family, friends, schoolmates, and workmates.

But we don't. We love other things more than peace. And we don't like anyone who tries to move us away from our primary loves in the name of peace.

I like how one of my favorite preachers summarizes the Beatitudes so far. She says, "Jesus is crazy!" Indeed, according to the world he's nuts. He is turning over the tables of so-called reality as he lays this foundation for his new community. How can this ever work?

THE PERFECT PLACE TO SAY THIS

Jesus is sitting at an elevation above the northwestern shoreline of the Sea of Galilee. He's talking about peacemakers.

What a fitting spot to do that. As he speaks, Jesus is literally in the middle of a chronic, non-stop war zone. One of the bloodiest places on earth. Jesus knows all about that legacy.

- 35 miles southwest in a broad valley 1500 years earlier the Egyptian King Tut III vanquished his Canaanite rivals.

• 300 years later it was the Israelites who defeated the Canaanites there (Judges 5).

• A generation later the Israelite Judge Gideon led the famous defeat and self-slaughter of the Midianites there (Judges 6-7).

• Israel's first king, Saul, was killed by the Philistines near there (I Samuel 31; II Samuel 1).

• 400 years later the Egyptians killed the young, charismatic King of Judah, Josiah (II Kings 23), leading to the ultimate destruction of Jerusalem and the Babylonian captivity twenty years later.

The valley is called Megiddo. Some call it Jezreel. It is also known as Armageddon, the envisioned sight of the final battle (Revelation 16—17).

And from there the ancient "Way of the Sea" slices right through where Jesus sits, giving passage to the Assyrian invasions, Roman legions, medieval Arab and Crusader armies, continuing to this day for would-be Syrian attackers pushed back in the 1973 Yom Kippur War.

Thus, we get the comment in Matthew chapter 4 following the report of Jesus' settling nearby in Capernaum:

> [14] *. . . so that what had been spoken through the prophet Isaiah might be fulfilled:* [15] *'Land of Zebulun, land of Naphtali, on the road by the sea, across the Jordan, Galilee of the Gentiles—* [16] *the people who sat in darkness have seen a great light, and for those who sat in the region and shadow of death light has dawned.'*

Blessed are the peacemakers, for they shall be called the children of God.

Jesus really is crazy. So are his people.

HOLD ON

But wait a minute, I thought Jesus said he didn't come to bring peace but a sword? Quoting again from Matthew 10, just five chapters later:

> [35]*"For I have come to set a man against his father, and a daughter against her mother, and a daughter-in-law against her mother-in-law;* [36] *and one's foes will be members of one's own household."*

Jesus did say all that. But in saying that he was not saying he came with the hope and ultimate goal of setting people against each other.

Rather, he was saying that this feature of conflict would be an inevitable effect of his coming.

He was controversial. He was a threat to people's established ways and will. He still is.

Not everybody liked him. Those who didn't and don't like him want to remove him. They want him and his people out of the picture. They work to get him and them out of their face and out of their space, coercively at times. They prefer their self-serving division and conflict rather than reconciliation with God and each other.

Jesus' life, message and actions will bring conflict due to resistance and hatred of what he stands for and who he is. What he stands for and who he is call for a kind of surrender in us. We don't want to give that.

But at the same time, who he is – life, message, actions – does bring life, peace and healed relationships. Well, it does to those who want that, to those who do surrender to him.

And that in time turns them into peacemakers themselves.

DEFINITIONS

Let's take a step back and ask a basic question. What is peace, and thus, peacemaking?

Eirene (pronounced eye-RAY-nay) is the Greek word here. We get the name "Irene" and the adjective "irenic" (bringing a peaceful approach to things) from this word.

Peace in the sense of *eirene* can describe both an inner state of tranquility, as well as an outer state of the absence of conflict.

But behind this Greek word is a Hebrew word and concept that is broader in scope. That word is the familiar *shalom* (pronounced sha-LOAM).

Shalom carries the sense of an entire circle of well-being in every direction, in every connection, arrangement and relationship in which your find yourself.*

You might say the individual is at the center of this circle, justly and rightly related to every point within and on the rim of the circle.

The circle embraces every dimension of reality that touches you, every relation and involvement: family, friends, neighbors, workmates, schoolmates, people at the gym, civic engagement, school board, local

---

*This is inspired by Dale Bruner's comment in *The Christbook: A Historical/Theological Commentary, Matthew 1-12;* Word Books: Waco, TX, 1987, pp. 149-150, and confirmed in the relevant lexicons.

food pantry, church ministries, mission efforts, wherever you leave your fingerprints and footprints . . . even with the physical environment. (Are you changing the oil in your car and dumping it in the side yard or disposing of it properly?!)

This circle of peace embraces your own self – spirit, soul and body. Are you taking care of the body God gave you? Are you tending to your own soul?

Soul. Now we're right at our center and right up against God.

What about your relationship with God? This is the all-encompassing relationship in this circle of peace, this *shalom* we are talking about. *Shalom* – everything where it ought to be, as it should be, according to the ways and the will of God.

THE PROBLEM WITH CIRCLES

That circle of peace in all of it relationships, in each and every direction, can have some bent and broken segments to it.

Our world likes the circle bent and warped both to its own advantage and to the disadvantage of the other.

The circle needs to be trued, brought into alignment. People are to be brought back into right relation to each other, to God, to their surroundings and to themselves. All within the circle begs to be strengthened, reconciled and restored.

Injustices face a reckoning with the powerful meekness of Jesus and his people. All that is bowed and contorted meets unblinking courage mixed with mercy and grace, even sacrifice, on the part of those making things right.

This is the way of the peacemaker. To bring peace is to round out that crooked circle. Make it right and balanced and, well, beautiful.

Blessed are the circle rounders, the menders, the reconcilers.

Listen to this from the Apostle Paul:

[19]For in him all the fullness of God was pleased to dwell, [20]and through him God was pleased to reconcile to himself all things, whether on earth or in heaven, by making peace through the blood of his cross. **Colossians 1:19-20**

Have you ever seen a peacemaker at work?

This would be the perfect time for a story, an example. Oh, sure, we have St. Francis of Assisi, Mother Theresa, Dietrich Bonhoeffer, etc., but I'm thinking of a more normal, non-celebrity, run of the mill, regular person who is a peacemaker. Someone who habitually gets in the middle of it with people, sits the people down and brings the people together with each other and with God.

Okay, maybe with God, sure, we can think of some evangelistic type of person, but what about someone who also brings people together with each other – some normal person who is known for that.

I know such people. Do you? The ones I know don't want me talking about them.

If you are hungering and thirsting for righteousness and being filled up with it, mercy and purity of heart and peacemaking are the unavoidable outflow.

When you get close to Jesus and are filled up with him, you just can't stop yourself. You can't not be a peacemaker.

Of course, you have to start with your own family and the immediate people around you. Otherwise, you're a pretender, a poser. This is the most difficult of work. It will cost you. And with your family, success is often far from guaranteed.

Everything else is a side show in comparison to peacemaking.

BETTER KNOWN SUMMARIES

Here are some visions of peacemaking from several who lived in the middle of conflict on a regular basis.

1) The conclusion of *Lincoln's Second Inaugural Address* at the close of the American Civil War:

> With malice toward none, with charity for all, with firmness in the right as God gives us to see the right, let us strive on to finish the work we are in, to bind up the nation's wounds, to care for him who shall have borne the battle and for his widow and his orphan, to do all which may achieve and cherish a just and lasting peace among ourselves and with all nations.

Notice the charity, firmness in what is right, care for soldiers and widows and orphans but not distinguishing sides. Notice the mercy-dominated justice tied to peace.

2) The famous *Prayer of St Francis of Assisi:*

> Lord, make me an instrument of your peace.
> Where there is hatred, let me bring love.
> Where there is offense, let me bring pardon.
> Where there is discord, let me bring union.
> Where there is error, let me bring truth.
> Where there is doubt, let me bring faith.
> Where there is despair, let me bring hope.
> Where there is darkness, let me bring your light.
> Where there is sadness, let me bring joy.
>
> O Master, let me not seek as much
> to be consoled as to console,
> to be understood as to understand,
> to be loved as to love,
> for it is in giving that one receives,
> it is in self-forgetting that one finds,
> it is in pardoning that one is pardoned,
> it is in dying that one is raised to eternal life.

Oh, that's sounding crazy like Jesus again. Yeah, and we are in need of a whole bunch of run-of-the-mill, every day, crazy people.

What is keeping you from being that?

Blessed are the peacemakers, for they will be called "children of God." They will be called that, because they are that.

Who calls them that? If not their "Father," then it really doesn't matter.

But he does, so it matters. And their peacemaking is the verification of their new name.

How blessed, how favored are they!

And now from St. Paul's second letter to the Corinthian Christians:

[16]From now on, therefore, we regard no one from a human point of view; even though we once knew Christ from a human point of view, we know him no longer in that way.

[17]So if anyone is in Christ, there is a new creation: everything old has passed away; see, everything has become new!

[18]All this is from God, who reconciled us to himself through Christ, and has given us the ministry of reconciliation; 19that is, in Christ God was reconciling the world to himself, not counting their trespasses against them, and entrusting the message of reconciliation to us.

[20]So we are ambassadors for Christ, since God is making his appeal through us; we entreat you on behalf of Christ, be reconciled to God. [21]For our sake he made him to be sin who knew no sin, so that in him we might become the righteousness of God. **II Corinthians 5:16-21**

I'm getting echoes of our beatitude passage all over the place in the above! We are not only given peace, now we go make it!

WHAT IT IS AND WHAT IT ISN'T

This ministry of reconciliation, this peacemaking work is not to be confused with appeasement. This is not pseudo-peacemaking at any price that papers over injustice, threatens healthy relationships and compromises integrity of being and life.

We are speaking of true peacemaking. Peacemaking that names things for what they are and calls everyone out into the open to fess up.

True peacemaking is not easy, and it doesn't come cheap. True peacemaking cost Jesus a lot through his life and ultimately led to his death. Peace was made with a cross and in no other way.

The denial of self and following in the way of the Crucified One provides the path for the true peacemaker.*

True peace and true forgiveness are therefore costly treasures purchased at great price. A cheap peace purchased with half-truths and cheap forgiveness brings more trouble, more pain and no reconciliation. In the words of Bonhoeffer, that would be a kind of "faith without repentance," a "faith without discipleship." That would be a cheap grace and really no grace at all.

We'll see some of the cost of peacemaking in the next beatitude.

INSEPARABLE

And now mercy, purity of heart and peacemaking remain, these three; and the greatest of these is . . .?

No, they are more like a trinity, a three-in-one. One fruit, three separate

---

*Jesus as peacemaker: Luke 2:14; 19:38; Acts 10:36; Rom 5:1; Eph 2:14-18; Col 1:2; Heb 7:2.

distinctions within the one. The three are in relationship and work together. You don't get one without the other two. They are a unity in their distinctions.

They are the gospel applied to us and then issuing from us. They are the expression of righteousness that fills us and then flows out of us.

HOW IS THIS A WRECKING BALL?

Simple.

This threefold outflow of mercy, purity of heart and peacemaking is devastating.

It is a direct challenge to the dark and evil arrangements of all that is wrong with the world.

It unmasks the abuse and enslavement of people.

It names and calls out racism wherever it resides.

It upsets, un-does and breaks down the way things are.

Those who profit from and are invested in a malevolent status quo don't want anything to change.

They do their best to stop it.

And that leads us to our final beatitude.

8

BLESSED: AFTER-ALL-THIS-AND-BECAUSE-OF-ALL-THIS, ALL-POSSESSING PERSECUTED ONES

[10]'Blessed are those who are persecuted for righteousness' sake, for theirs is the kingdom of heaven.'

Matthew 5:10

[11]'Blessed are you when people revile you and persecute you and utter all kinds of evil against you falsely on my account. [12]Rejoice and be glad, for your reward is great in heaven, for in the same way they persecuted the prophets who were before you.'

Matthew 5:11-12

THIS IS SURPRISING!

"Rejoice and be glad, . . ."???

Really?

Yes, really.

You are rewarded, now and later.

THIS IS TIMELY

If this isn't a word for our time, I don't know what is.

In recent years we've heard of mass graves and ongoing testimonies of ethnic and religious cleansing by groups such as ISIS – conforming to the slogan of radical jihadists "First the Saturday people (Jews) then the Sunday people (Christians.)"

As recently as January 2021 the Christian NGO, Open Doors published its annual "World Watch List." The reporting period was from October 2019 through September 2020. Worldwide, 340 million Christians were living in countries with the risk of high levels of persecution and discrimination, with 309 million of this number in danger of very high levels of persecution. Open Doors noted this represents 1 in 8 Christians worldwide, 1 in 6 in Africa, 2 in 5 in Asia, and 1 in 12 in Latin America.*

Some say the 20th century saw more Christians die for their faith than all previous centuries combined. It hasn't gotten any better as our 21st

---

*"One In Eight Christians Worldwide Live In Countries Where They May Face Persecution," *Forbes* / January 13, 2021 / Ewelina U. Ochab.

century continues to unfold.

And what of increasingly hostile environments in the supposedly tolerant West: incrementally (or not-so-incrementally) challenging and restricting freedoms by means of legislation; corporate market control, media, Big Tech, racially based injustices; anti-life movements; and "politically-correct" pressure?

UNFORGETTABLE MOMENT

I'm reminded of one of my graduate school professors who was born and raised in Germany. In the late 1930s at the age of eight he found himself in the "Hitler Youth" organization. Every "ethnically pure" boy in the Germany of that time was automatically included. No other option was given.

He belonged to a Methodist family. They hated the Nazis.

On November 9-10, 1938 *Kristallnacht* (the night of shattered glass) saw 1000 synagogues and 700 businesses destroyed or damaged with more than one hundred dead, and estimates of 30,000 Jewish men sent into early versions of Nazi concentration camps.

My professor walked to church as usual with his family the following Sunday morning. Nazi storm troopers in their brown shirts were still milling around the smoldering ruins of the local synagogue – just across the alley from the side entrance to their church where his family always entered. One of the troopers approached him, leaned down and with his finger pointing announced, "You're next!"

First the Saturday people, then the Sunday people.

WHY ALL THE FUSS?

'Blessed are those who are persecuted for righteousness' sake.'

Righteousness fills up the true Sunday people to overflowing and spills out of them onto everyone and everything around them. This gets the Sunday people in trouble. Trouble comes for the "sake" of this righteousness, on account of this righteousness, because of concrete expressions of this righteousness . . .

- Mercy extended towards others;
- Pure hearts seeking the will of God in all things, nothing more, nothing less, nothing else;
- Peacemaking that speaks the truth and brings people together, reconciling enemies.

Jesus is saying in so many words, "All this righteousness will be seen as a direct threat, as a challenge, as an assault upon the powers that be."

"The System," the established order, the so-called "world" does not like "righteousness" (as defined in the Beatitudes) one bit. That world benefits from the absence of mercy, puts itself in the place of God in the hearts of people, and thrives on the absence of peace . . . on conflict that keeps people divided.

WHOM ARE WE TALKING ABOUT?

On a larger scale and in more extreme forms we're talking about unjust government getting irritated with followers of Jesus. Government that:

- sets up a status quo serving a privileged set;
- throws its weight around, dominating people, using people, with no care for the interests of people;
- shows no commitment to justice and fair play for people, for setting things right, especially if it means losing its own position and power over the people.

But the above can range from corrupt regimes all the way down to couples in a dating relationship. For example:

- Herod's kingdom in 1st century Palestine;
- the Jerusalem religious establishments of Jesus' day;
- certain Roman Catholic dioceses protecting child-abusing priests in recent days;
- self-serving, high-profile leaders in Protestant churches and their networks;
- corrupt religious orders and groups;
- cultural traditions that keep people ignorant and repressed;
- civil servants who serve themselves;
- crime syndicates and armed gangs;
- administrative bureaucracies committed to self-preservation;
- corporate interests shaping social opinion through distorted news and storylines;
- school boards that are about power and not children;
- grassroots organizations with dark agendas;

- status quo "good-old-boy" networks;
- broken down neighborhoods and the people who keep them that way;
- families that control their members;
- sick and abusive relationships between two people.

On a grand scale or on a small scale we are talking about humanity that arranges itself according to its own interests and against the interests of God.

We are talking about the potential in each one of us to seek exclusive advantage over the rest.

But now all these are threatened by Jesus' presence and Jesus' words embodied in you and me – merciful, pure-hearted peacemakers posing a question and a challenge to the way things are.

"The world" doesn't like that, wants to remove that, wants to remove you! The world's response is persecution, pushback and attack.

A HEADS UP

Jesus says, "Expect this! Don't be surprised at this. It's coming."

Death and Taxes? Yes, but better add a third to the list of what is certain in life – persecution. This is as sure as the other two when it comes to Jesus' people . . . when they are truly being Jesus' people.

The good news is that persecuted ones are blessed ones. '*Blessed* are those who are persecuted for righteousness' sake, . . ."

Why? They get the Kingdom of Heaven.

COMING FULL CIRCLE

This is the second of two bookends.

"Those who are persecuted for righteousness' sake" are the same people we started with back in the first Beatitude. Remember?

The "poor in spirit" are the ones who get the "Kingdom of Heaven" right off the bat. They then get filled with righteousness which then flows out from them and gets the world system all worked up and anxious and upset. All for good reason. Its days are numbered. It is brittle. It will come to an end, and it doesn't like facing that.

Jesus' people pay a price for pointing that out, for getting in the way, for spoiling the party. We pay a price. But it's worth the price.

The "poor in spirit" in the beginning wind up being "those who are persecuted" in the end. Both get "the kingdom." The identical phrase is used to explain why both are blessed – *'for theirs is the kingdom of heaven.'* Same person, from start to finish. This is the story of a transformed life.

And, also, remember that same person gets a share in that kingdom both now and later in all its fullness. That's what it means when it says the kingdom "is" (present tense) "theirs" (possessive).

PERSECUTED ONES IN TURKEY

On the morning of April 18, 2007, I was living in Istanbul and taking a Turkish lesson. We suddenly got word of some violence out east in the city of Malatya (mah-LOT-yah).

Three Christian workers, two of them Turks and the other a German, that very morning had been bound, abused and then murdered by young men pretending to participate in a Bible study exploring Christianity. We knew the victims.

The fledging Turkish Christian Movement had now been baptized into the ranks of a persecuted church.

Whether the murderers – all five of them under 23 years of age at the time – or the ones who put them up to it understood Christianity is open to question. What they did understand, and what is always true of opposition to righteousness is that righteousness and anyone associated with it are seen as a threat to the way things are. For the powers-that-be that's a non-starter.

There are, of course, many stories of less dramatic but very real pressure applied to Turkish Christians. See if you can relate to any of the following:

- a young couple is cut off from the family and cut out of the family will – they have disgraced the family, rejected Islam, joined "the religion of the enemy";
- a young man loses his teaching job, accused of being a missionary – reckoned in the same category of intrigue and adversarial intent as a CIA agent;
- a teenage girl is prevented by her father from attending the youth

group at the Turkish church;
• my Turkish roommate keeps his faith secret from his family for fear of his radicalized uncles inflicting harm upon him;
• a thoroughly secularized young man finds Jesus, but his secular Turkish parents threaten to take legal action to disown him.

Association with the name of Jesus and the righteousness that comes with the name, labels them, and they pay for it.

PERSECUTED ONES IN AMERICA

Let's get a little closer to home:

• a vice chancellor of a top-tier university says to a Presbyterian pastor friend that if you are a professor in the humanities and it becomes known you are a Christian, your career is finished;
• you refuse to cut corners at work and lie for the boss, and maybe *your* career is finished;
• you bring up Jesus at Thanksgiving and get the silent treatment;
• you recommend to your family mercy toward an "enemy," but are shut down, made fun of, become the subject of gossip and ridicule;
• you extend hospitality to a stereotyped foreigner across the street, and the neighbors shun you;
• you suggest past complicity of many churches in the history of slavery and racism in America and you are ostracized;
• you make noise about an injustice and you yourself then receive an unjust reaction for it;
• you become a Christian and your significant other responds by

dumping you, or your marriage is thrown into a crisis.

I could go on.

THAT SURPRISE AGAIN

Here is Jesus' response in so many words (verses 11-12):

> *Blessed are you . . . Rejoice and be glad . . . Great is your reward in heaven . . . That's how they always treat the righteous. That's how they treated the prophets. That's how they are now and will continue to treat me.*

"If that's how they treat me, that's how they will treat you. And if that's how they treat you, you'll know you are in good company, on the right path, headed for something good, a great reward. (This, of course, requires faith, hope and a strong love for God.)"

And how about this: If there is no persecution in your life, no ridicule, no false accusation on his account of any kind, if your life is not ever making anyone uncomfortable, what does that say?

Is there any righteousness coming out of you that is upsetting any unjust, ungodly thing or behavior in another?

Another question: Is it possible for supposed "Christians" – more committed to their own comfortable system than to the Jesus of the Beatitudes – to hassle, obstruct, even persecute real followers of Jesus? Followers who are all about extending mercy, seeking God, and settling for nothing less, being peacemakers inside and outside the church?

Yes, it is. I've seen it happen. So have you.

SUMMING IT UP

A Beatitude life is full of blessing but will get you into trouble.

Being different disturbs what wants to stay the same.

Darkness hates light.

Back to you and me. Do you know the saying, "If it were against the law to be a Christian, would there be enough evidence to convict you"?

Well, would there be? Are you a known Christian? I don't mean because you are obnoxious about it and can't shut up. I mean are you known, because while the evidence of Jesus in you and the actions of Jesus through you bless many, they also may make other people feel uncomfortable to the point of reaction?

Try offering mercy in a situation where everyone else wants to execute judgement on someone. Try not participating in the gossip around you and even discouraging it. Try making peace between parties in conflict who do not want peace and see what you get.

But remember . . .

> [10]*'Blessed are those who are persecuted for righteousness' sake, for theirs is the kingdom of heaven.'*
>
> **Matthew 5:10**

No one can take that away from you.

CONCLUSION

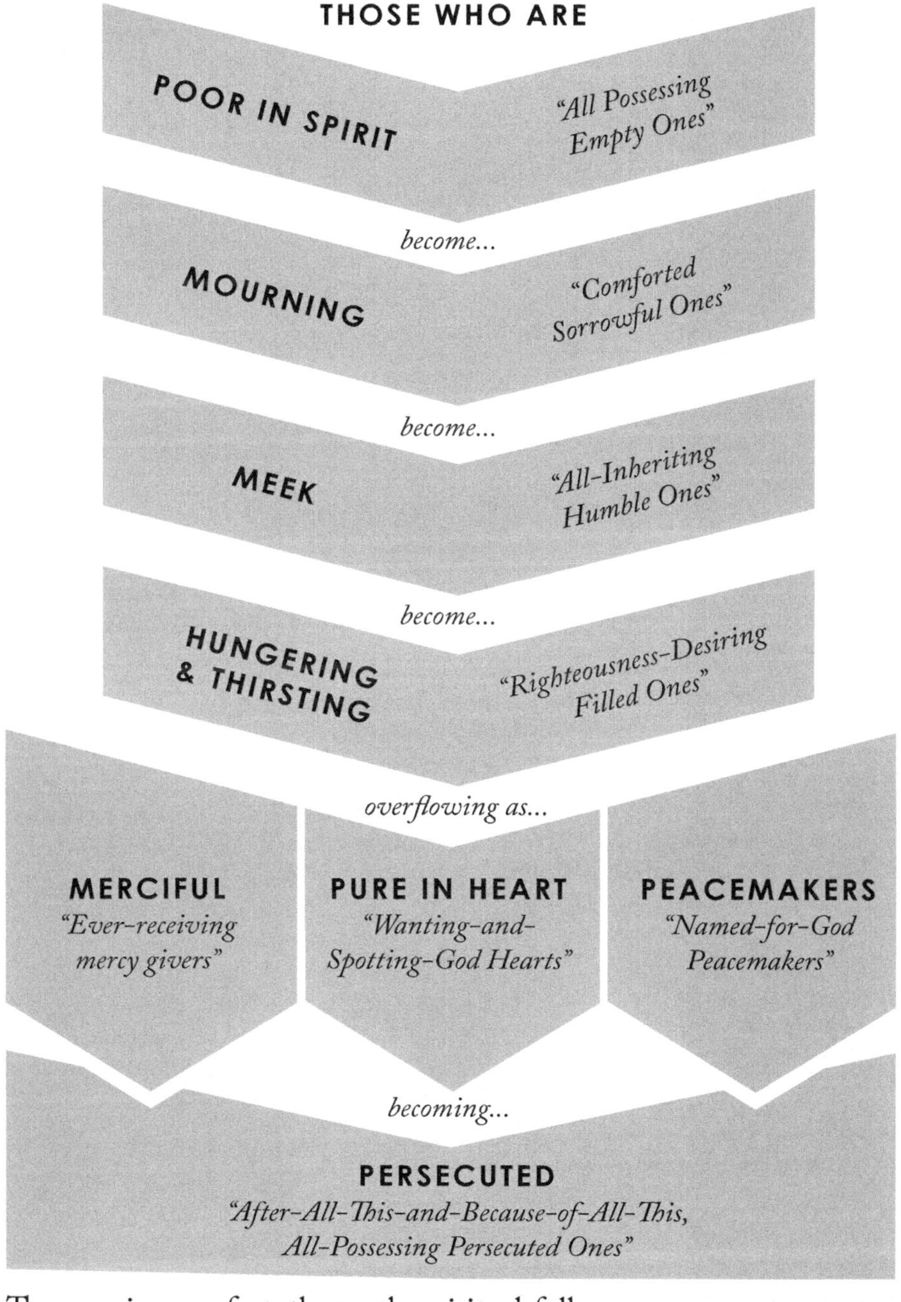

They receive comfort, the earth, spiritual fullness, mercy, an awareness of God, adoption by God, the Kingdom of Heaven.

It is the greatest and most expansive, blessed life possible.

APPENDICES

1. FURTHER READING

Dietrich Bonhoeffer, *The Cost of Discipleship*, New York, 1995.

Dale Bruner, *Matthew, A Commentary: The Christbook – Matthew 1-12*, Grand Rapids, 2004.

W.D. Davies & D.C. Allison, *Matthew 1-7* (ICC), London, 1988.

Robert Gundry, *Matthew: A Commentary on His Literary and Theological Art*, Grand Rapids, 1982.

Martyn Lloyd-Jones, *Studies in the Sermon on the Mount*, Grand Rapids, 1971 & 1976.

Jacques Philippe, *Interior Freedom*, Burtin, France, 2002.

2. ACKNOWLEDGEMENTS

The following represent environments and relationships both influencing and receiving the evolving content of this book over the last 40+ years: Westmont College / Santa Barbara, CA; Westminster Presbyterian Church of Hueneme / Port Hueneme, CA; Antalya Bible Church / Antalya, Turkey; Harvest Church Ministries / Istanbul, Turkey; Resurrection Church / Istanbul, Turkey; 1st Presbyterian Church / Downey, CA; Evangelical Covenant Order of Presbyterians; Klamath Falls Presbyterian Church / Klamath Falls, OR; 1st Presbyterian Church / Jerome, ID; Liberty Corner Presbyterian Church / Liberty Corner, NJ; 1st Presbyterian Church / Greenville, SC; Grace Presbyterian Church / Houston, TX; Christ Pacific Church / Huntington Beach, CA;

Glenkirk Church / Glendora, CA; Christ Community Church Milpitas (CCCM) / Milpitas, CA; Community Presbyterian Church / Ventura, CA; Dr. Robert Gundry; Rev. Ramazan Arkan; Pamela Schubert; George Bristow; Hanspeter Tiefenbach, John Terech, Rev. Karen Ballard; Rev. Jen Howat; Rev. Lisa Johnson; Rev. Amber Ayers; Rev. Stuart Bond; Rev. Peter Little; Rev. Gary Watkins; Rev. Trey Little; Rev. Chris French; Rev. Don Feuerbach; Rev. Anne Havrilla; Rev. Nate Dreesmann; Rev. Jenn Graffius; CCCM Wednesday Night Life Group / Milpitas, CA; Jon Obermeyer; Larry Warner, Leeba Lessin. Many thanks to Jezreal Gandara for initially locating some of the photos used, to Linda Terry for copy-editing the manuscript and to Cynthia Meyers for assisting in formatting and layout.

3. ENGAGING WITH ME: fearerttalk@gmail.com

4. AUTHOR BIO

Tim has pastored five churches, labored as a theological educator and leadership developer in the country of Turkey, and in more recent years committed himself to strengthening the life and work of pastors and elders throughout the United States. A certified coach and spiritual director, Tim holds several graduate degrees and currently takes short term pastorates for the Evangelical Covenant Order of Presbyterians, navigating congregations and their leadership teams through periods of transition. When not away on assignment Tim makes his home amidst the people, color and beauty of the Los Angeles basin.

Made in the USA
Middletown, DE
20 May 2022

65987715R00076